BEAT BULLYING

Honor Head

W
FRANKLIN WATTS
LONDON·SYDNEY

Published in paperback in Great Britain in 2020
by The Watts Publishing Group
© The Watts Publishing Group 2020

All rights reserved

Managing editor: Victoria Brooker
Design: Sophie Burdess

Image Credits: Shutterstock – all images Good Studio apart from aommaneesri 11ct, 11cb, 12t, 12br; Maksim Ankudua 11c; Tetiana Savaryn 20b

Every attempt has been made to clear copyright.
Should there be any inadvertent omission
please apply to the publisher for rectification.

ISBN: 9781445170640 (hbk)
ISBN: 9781445170657 (pbk)

Printed in China

Franklin Watts
An imprint of
Hachette Children's Group
Part of the Watts Publishing Group
Carmelite House
50 Victoria Embankment
London EC4Y 0DZ
An Hachette UK Company
www.hachette.co.uk
www.franklinwatts.co.uk

The website addresses (URLs) included in this book
were valid at the time of going to press.
However, it is possible that contents or addresses may
have changed since the publication of this book.
No responsibility for any such changes can be accepted
by either the author or the Publisher.

CONTENTS

WHAT IS BULLYING?		4
1.	UNDERSTAND CYBERBULLYING	6
2.	WIPE OUT BULLYING AT SCHOOL	8
3.	BE ASSERTIVE	10
4.	TAKE BACK YOUR POWER	12
5.	STAY SAFE	14
6.	BE SAFE ONLINE	16
7.	Deal with online nasties	18
8.	DEAL WITH BEING LEFT OUT	20
9.	Control PEER PRESSURE	22
10.	TAKE A TECH BREAK	24
11.	RECOGNISE FRENEMIES	26
12.	ask for help	28
Where to get help		30
Glossary		32

WHAT IS BULLYING?

Bullying is when someone deliberately and repeatedly makes you feel scared or threatened by words or their behaviour. It includes physical and mental harm. Bullying can happen at school, in public places and at home.

SAYING NASTY THINGS

PHYSICAL ASSAULT
such as hitting, punching, spitting, pinching, arm twisting.

BEING IGNORED

DAMAGING YOUR BELONGINGS

EMOTIONAL BULLYING

FORCING YOU TO DO THINGS YOU DON'T WANT TO

NO-ONE HAS A RIGHT TO HURT YOU OR MAKE YOU FEEL SCARED... NOT YOUR FRIENDS, YOUR TEACHERS, OR YOUR FAMILY.

BULLIES ARE COWARDS. THEY ENJOY HURTING PEOPLE. IT MAKES THEM FEEL BIG AND POWERFUL BUT REALLY THEY ARE WEAK.

1. UNDERSTAND CYBERBULLYING

Cyberbullying is people bullying on digital devices, such as smart phones, computers and tablets. They use Twitter, WhatsApp, Snapchat and other social networking sites and online forums to make people feel bad.

- Abusive messages, name calling, hate mail, trolling.
- Being blocked from online games or chat forums for no reason.
- Posting embarrassing photos or information.
- Starting false rumours that are upsetting or embarrassing.
- Impersonating someone online to send nasty messages.

Cyberbullying is constant ... it can happen every hour, every day, every week, wherever you are.

Even home isn't safe anymore...

Are you a cyberbully?

It can be easy to upset someone online without realising it.

- What might seem like a joke to you can really damage a person's self-esteem and confidence.

- A thoughtless message from you could encourage others to make abusive comments even if this isn't what you intended.

- Messaging something quickly in anger without thinking could get out of hand.

- Don't 'like' or share anything that is abusive, threatening or mean.

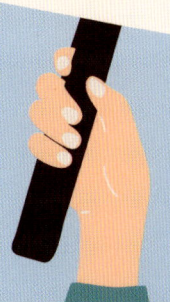

Always be aware of what you say and do online.

2. WIPE OUT BULLYING AT SCHOOL

Your school has a legal right to protect you from abuse and bullying and to make school a safe place. There are things you can do to help …

NO BULLY ZONE

Make a safe space where kids being bullied can go to talk to a teacher.

Stand up and support kids being bullied.

Create a school safety group with a teacher.

Make posters about bullying.

Treat people with respect!

Write a school play about bullying.

Do an assembly or classroom talk on bullying.

Being bullied?

Try this …

Avoid the areas where the bullies wait for you if you can.

Tell a teacher or other adult.

Find out the school rules against bullying.

No school rules against bullying? Work with teachers to create one and make sure everyone knows about it.

It is hard, but try and stand up to the bully. Stand tall, take a deep breathe, look them in the eye and say 'Stop!' or 'Go away!' in a firm voice.

If a bully is violent, stay away, don't fight back. You must tell a teacher, adult or the police.

3. BE ASSERTIVE

Bullies are cowards and will pick on people they think are weaker than themselves. Stand tall, look strong and beat the bullies.

GOOD BODY POSTURE

Having good body posture will help you to feel confident and might also make bullies think twice about picking on you.

Don't slouch

Don't look at the ground

Don't look fearful

Stand tall and straight

Don't fidget

Keep your head up

Smile and look confident

Look people in the eye

If you are being threatened by violence and need help – **SHOUT!** Breathe deeply and shout out from the very pit of your stomach **HELP!** or **NO!**

BEING ASSERTIVE IS NOT THE SAME AS BEING AGGRESSIVE.

AGGRESSIVE

- Fists clenched
- Shouting in face
- Leaning forward menacingly
- Getting angry

ASSERTIVE

- Arms by side
- Firm but normal voice
- Staying in your own space
- Staying calm

FIGHT ANGER

Being bullied can make you feel stressed and angry all the time. Here's what to do:

- Aerobic exercise - helps burn up your angry energy
- Thump a pillow or cushion in your room
- Shout or scream into a pillow or cushion
- Breathe deeply for a few minutes
- Write down what has made you angry, screw it up and throw it away.

4. TAKE BACK YOUR POWER

You are powerful and strong …

sometimes you just need to try a few techniques to find your power.

I've got the power!

Step 5 — Every day, think of 5 things to be grateful for, such as a sunny day or fun times with friends.

Step 4 — List 5 skills that you have, such as being able to whistle tunes or knit.

Step 3 — List 5 things you like about how you look, such as great hair or fabulous smile.

Step 2 — List 5 positive things that make you unique and special, such as being kind and a good listener.

Step 1 — Stop comparing yourself with others.

5. STAY SAFE

Bullies and gangs can be dangerous. If you feel threatened, travel in a group or ask an adult to collect you. Avoid quiet places after dark.

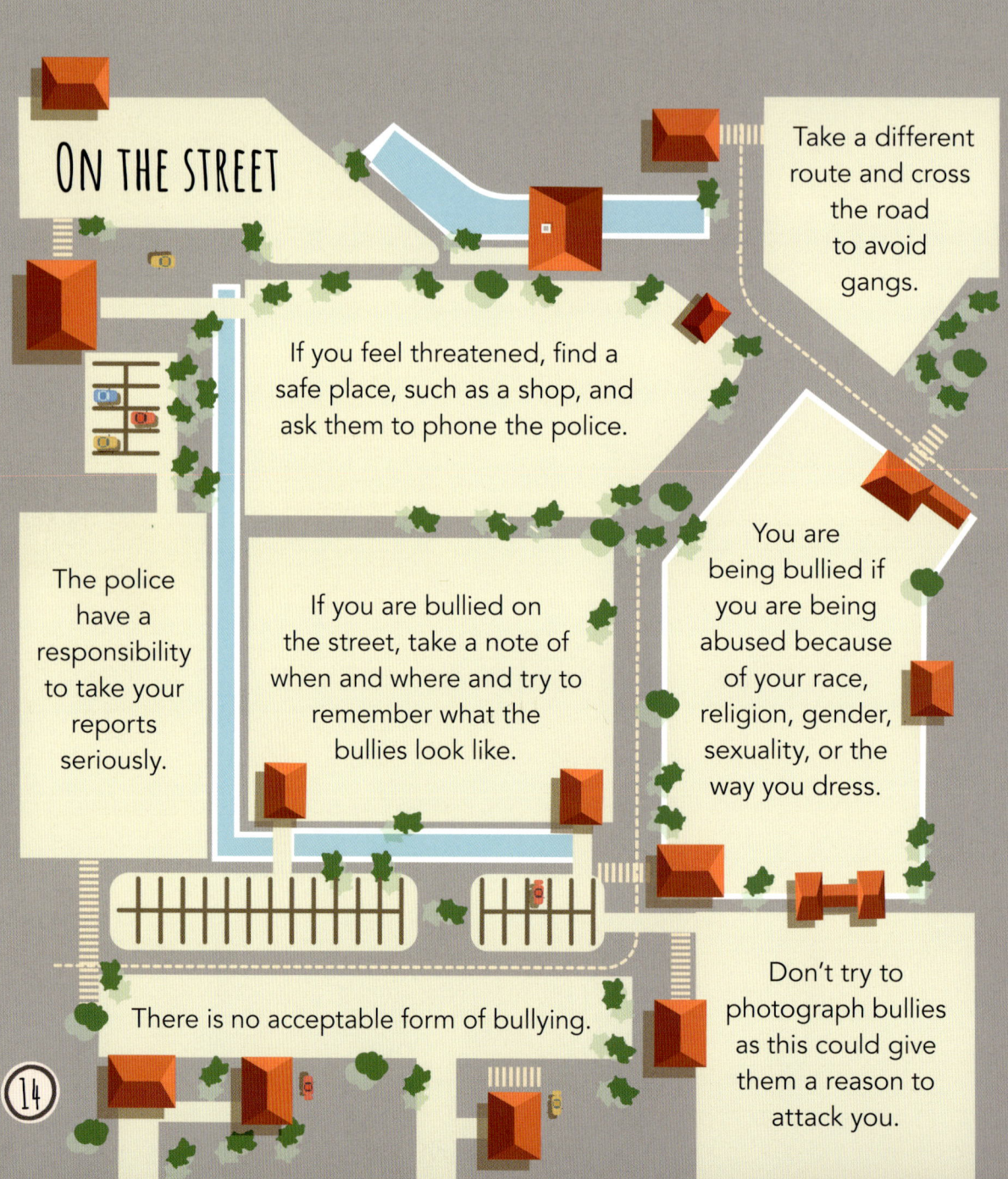

On the street

Take a different route and cross the road to avoid gangs.

If you feel threatened, find a safe place, such as a shop, and ask them to phone the police.

The police have a responsibility to take your reports seriously.

If you are bullied on the street, take a note of when and where and try to remember what the bullies look like.

You are being bullied if you are being abused because of your race, religion, gender, sexuality, or the way you dress.

There is no acceptable form of bullying.

Don't try to photograph bullies as this could give them a reason to attack you.

AT HOME

No adult has a right to harm you physically, mentally or emotionally. Not your family, your friends or your teachers.

You shouldn't ever feel guilty for reporting bullying.

If you are being bullied at home, speak to a trusted adult, the police or phone a helpline.

It is your right to feel safe on the street and at home.

6. BE SAFE ONLINE

Follow some basic rules to help keep cyberbullies away.

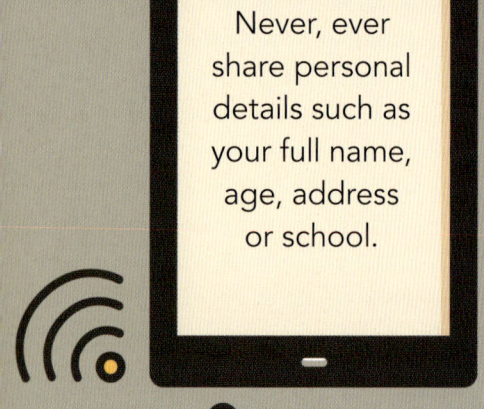

Never, ever share personal details such as your full name, age, address or school.

Always make sure you get permission before posting a photo with anyone else in it.

Photos stay online forever. Be careful what you post online. Make sure you don't mind any photos you post being seen by your parents, carers, teachers and future employers.

Keep photos and videos for trusted friends and family only.

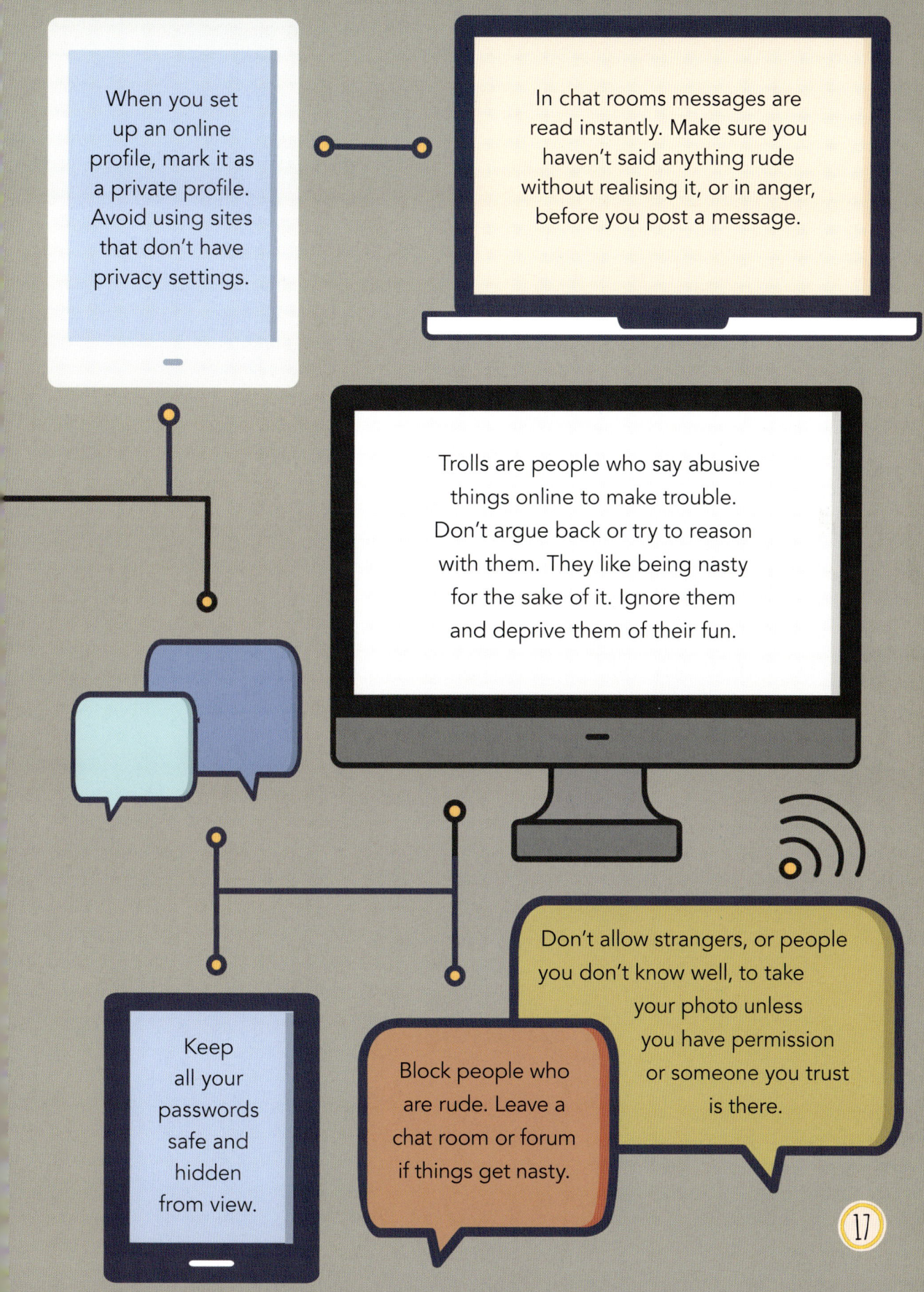

7. DEAL WITH ONLINE NASTIES

The police take online bullying, sexting and sites that encourage dangerous behaviour very seriously. If you come across anything like this, you should tell an adult immediately.

Most sites have a report abuse button – use it if you need to.

SWITCH OFF
Take a break and give online bullies the cold shoulder – turn off your devices for a while.

Tell an adult if you are being cyberbullied or being sent rude messages or texts. You or the adults should keep screenshots of abusive mail and images that might be useful if you report the bullying.

You should never feel you have to put up with online nasties because you think it is your fault. Speak to an adult about the issues and deal with it together.

Sexting is sending sexually explicit photos, videos or other content on digital devices. This material stays online forever and could end up going viral.

If someone is sending you sexually explicit and embarrassing material, tell an adult. Do not respond or pass on the material. If you can, keep it to show the police.

If anyone asks for photos that you find embarrassing or rude, tell an adult straight away.

Some online sites can be very upsetting. They show people harming themselves, starving themselves and some can encourage life-threatening behaviour. Talk to an adult or a helpline if you are being affected by a site like this.

8. DEAL WITH BEING LEFT OUT

Being left out or excluded deliberately from social media sites is a form of cyberbullying.

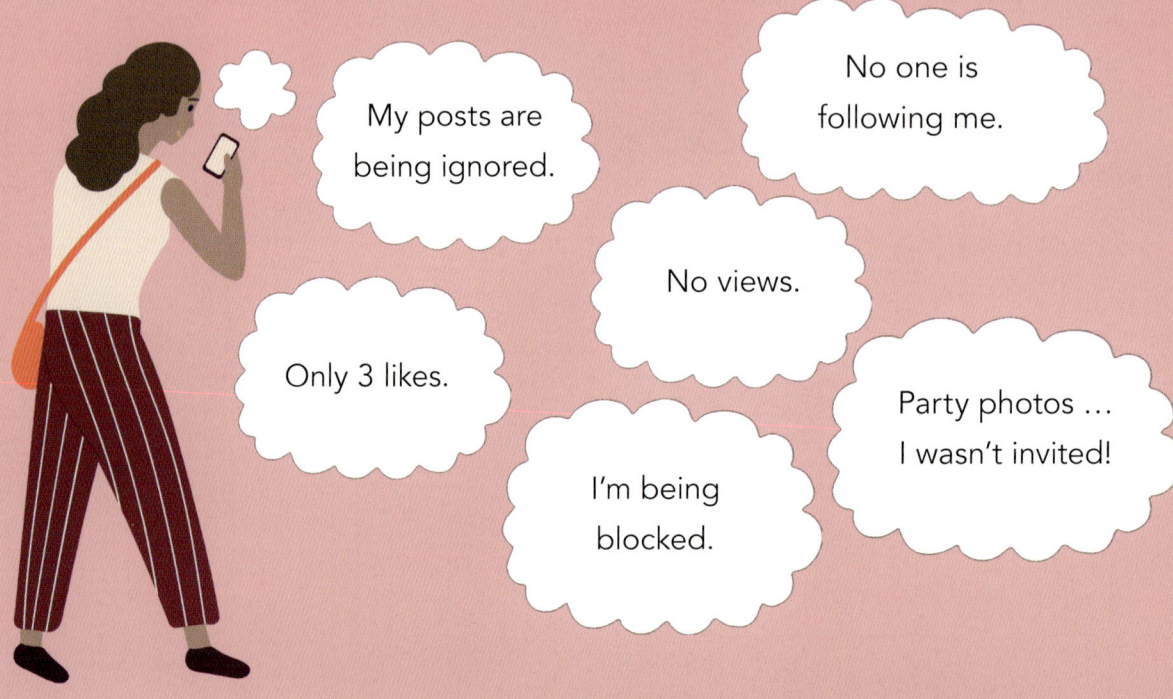

- My posts are being ignored.
- No one is following me.
- No views.
- Only 3 likes.
- I'm being blocked.
- Party photos … I wasn't invited!

Don't allow other people to make you feel bad about yourself. Just because you have been excluded by bullies doesn't make you bad, boring or not good enough. Find another way, your own way.

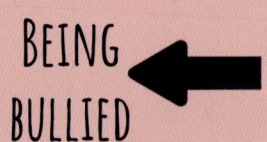

Being blocked and ignored can make you feel insecure, alone and isolated. If it is being done deliberately think why.

Did you post something that upset someone?

YES

Apologise and it should pass. Everyone makes mistakes.

Check what you say in future before posting.

NO

Why you are being left out? Maybe you said or posted something upsetting without realising it.

Take a tech break. Watch a film, read, listen to your favourite music, chat with the family.

Real friends wouldn't exclude you for no reason. Think about joining a new club and finding a different chat site.

9. CONTROL PEER PRESSURE

Peer pressure is when you feel that you have to do something because your friends or classmates are doing it. Don't be forced into doing what you don't want to do.

STOP! THINK!

Think: would a real friend ask you to do anything that was illegal, dangerous or embarrassing?

Think: what might happen if you do this? You could get arrested or be injured. What would your family think if that happened?

Be brave, be true to yourself and say no!

Talk to an adult if things are getting out of hand or if you feel threatened.

Block or turn off sites that pressure you into doing illegal or dangerous things.

People who force you to do things you don't want to are not friends, they are bullies. Doing things you don't really want to won't make you happy or feel good.

10. TAKE A TECH BREAK

It may not be as difficult as you think ... try it for an hour, a morning or evening, a day and then a week.

What will I do instead?

Film Society

help Wildlife

Music

Sport

Look for local groups or clubs to join

Book Club

Art

Choir

See if there is a local group that helps clear up litter, plants trees or looks after the local environment.

Organise events with your friends … meet for a regular dance session, go for walks or to play football in the park, get together to make pizzas, watch films or just enjoy talking and being together.

Go for walks or play games with the family – it could be fun!

Learn something new, such as painting, a new sport, karate … it will make you feel smarter and you'll meet new people.

Keep a journal about how you coped with your tech-free time!

11. RECOGNISE FRENEMIES

The word is a mix of friend and enemy – you get the picture!

A FRENEMY PRETENDS TO BE YOUR FRIEND BUT:

- talks about you behind your back

- betrays secrets and confidences and says it was an accident

- makes you do things you don't want to because you're best mates

- is not trustworthy

- teases you in front of other people in a way that makes you feel bad

- excludes you from stuff

- says mean things 'as a joke'.

It is difficult to let go of a person we think is a friend, but if a friend doesn't support you and make you feel good, are they worth keeping?

How to stand up to a frenemy:

- Believe you deserve a better sort of friendship.

- Know it's okay to be angry but not aggressive. Tell the person firmly, but calmly, what they have done to hurt you and say you won't put up with it again.

- Take action! If it keeps happening, move away from that person or group. Look for other friends and things to do. It might be hard to begin with, but finding real friends is worth the effort.

12. ASK FOR HELP

Everyone needs help at times for lots of different reasons. It is not being weak or stupid or silly to ask for help. It is brave and smart to ask for help when things get a bit too much. Learn to recognise when you should ask for help.

Ask for help when:

- you feel overwhelmed 
- you can't sleep
- your school work is being affected
- you feel angry all the time
- you can't cope

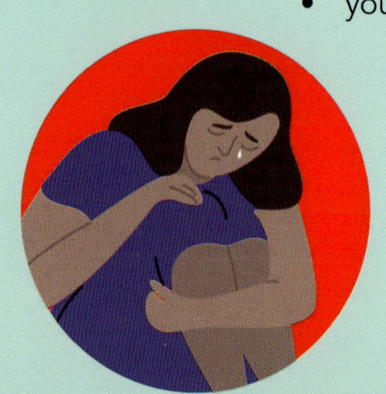

- you don't want to see friends
- you are hurting yourself

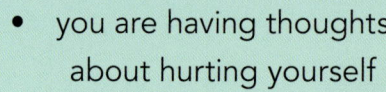

- you are having thoughts about hurting yourself
- you feel scared, anxious or sad all the time.

Who to ask:

If you can, speak to a trusted adult such as a parent or carer, aunt, grandparent, coach, or teacher. Choose a quiet time and say you have something important to tell them. If you prefer, write your thoughts down and hand it to the person you trust.

Join an online forum with others who may be going through something similar to you. Talking with others can help you realise you are not alone.

Phone a helpline – there are some listed on the next page. No one will be shocked or embarrassed about what you say and they won't judge you.

YOU DESERVE HELP. JUST ASK!

WHERE TO GET HELP

If you feel that worry is taking over your life or you have lots of panic attacks or anxiety, you must speak to someone. Try and talk to your carers, a trusted adult, a teacher or your friends about how you feel. If there is no one you want to talk to, there are loads of places online that can help you. Chat rooms and forums are great for talking to people who feel the same way as you do and may have had similar experiences. However, never share personal details with anyone, no matter how genuine they seem. Never meet up with strangers.

Telephone helplines are places where you can talk to someone who is specially trained to understand what you are going through. They won't judge you or make you do anything you don't want to do. You don't have to be embarrassed or feel ashamed or silly about what you tell them. They will be understanding, kind and supportive.

www.childline.org.uk/info-advice/yourfeelings/mental-health
Message or call the 24 hour helpline
for advice or someone who'll just listen.
The helpline is 0800 1111

https://papyrus-uk.org
A place to go if you have bad thoughts
about harming yourself or suicide.
HopelineUK 0800 068 41 41

www.samaritans.org
A place where anyone can go for
advice and comfort.
The helpline is 08457 90 90 90

www.sane.org/get-help
Help and support for anyone affected
by mental and emotional issues.
The helpline is 0300 304 7000

www.supportline.org.uk
A charity giving emotional support to young people.
The helpline is 01708 765200

kidshealth.org/en/kids/feeling
Advice on managing emotions.

www.youngminds.org.uk
Advice for young people experiencing bullying, stress and mental or emotional anxieties.

kidshealth.org.uk
A site dedicated to helping keep kids safe from bullying.

SHOUT!
A text only 24/7 helpline for anyone suffering from emotional and mental issues or going through a crisis.
Text 85258 and a trained volunteer will be there to help.

Or settle down with a book...

Dealing with Bullying by Jane Lacey, Franklin Watts, 2019

Say No to Bullying by Louise Spilsbury, Wayland, 2015

Bullies, Cyberbullies and Frenemies by Michele Elliot, Wayland, 2013

GLOSSARY

aerobic exercise that makes your heart beat faster
betrays lets your down; is not loyal
confidence feeling you can do something well
explicit in great detail
illegal against the law
impersonating pretending to be someone else
insecure feeling uncertain and anxious
positive feeling confident and hopeful
respect treating someone well because you admire them
self-esteem the way you feel about yourself and your ability to do things
sexting sending someone sexually explicit photos or messages
unique one of a kind

INDEX

aggression 11, 26, 27
anxiety 28
assertiveness 10–11

breathing 9, 11

clubs 21, 24
comparisons 12, 13
computers 6
cyberbullying 6–7, 16–17, 19

digital devices 6, 19

emotional bullying 5, 15
exclusion 4, 6, 20–21, 26
exercise 11, 24, 25

family 15, 25
friends 15, 20–21, 23, 25, 26–27, 28

gangs 14
gender 14

hate mail 6, 19
helplines 15, 29
home 4, 7, 15

impersonation 6

messages 6, 17, 19

name calling 6

online 6–7, 16–17
 forums 6, 17, 29
 games 6
 passwords 17
 posting 20–21
 profile 17

peer pressure 22–23
personal details 16
photos 6, 14, 16, 17, 19, 22
police 9, 14, 15, 18, 19
positivity 12–13
posture 10
public places 4, 14
race 14
religion 14

reporting 15, 18–19, 23
rules 9, 16
rumours 6

safe places 8, 14
scared, feeling 4, 28
school 4, 8–9, 16, 28
screenshots 19
self-harm 19, 28
sexting 18, 19
sexuality 14
sleep 28
social networks 6, 20
sport 24, 25

talking 27
teachers 8, 9, 15, 29
tech breaks 21, 24–25
trolls 6, 17

videos 16, 19
violence 9, 10
viral 19

words 4, 9, 10
writing 11, 29